Easy
Cupcake
Recipes

Cookbook Resources, LLC
Highland Village, Texas

Easy Cupcake Recipes

Printed September 2011

International Standard Book Number: 978-1-59769-045-4

Library of Congress Control Number: 2010022620

Library of Congress Cataloging-in-Publication Data

       Easy cupcake recipes.
          p. cm.
       Includes index.
       ISBN 978-1-59769-045-4
       1. Cupcakes.
       TX771.E204 2010
       641.8'653--dc22

                                  2010022620

Cover and illustrations by Rasor Designs and Nancy Bohanan

Edited, Designed and Published in the United States of America and Manufactured in China by
Cookbook Resources, LLC
541 Doubletree Drive
Highland Village, Texas 75077

Toll free 866-229-2665

www.cookbookresources.com

cookbook
≋resources® LLC
Bringing Family and Friends to the Table

Fun for the Whole Family!

How much fun... you're 10 years old and there's not an adult in sight! (That's because when you make cupcakes and decorate them, you can be whatever age you want to be.)

Whatever excuse you want to use is enough to make cupcakes... daughter's birthday, son scored a goal, your dad's retirement, a neighborhood party... any excuse will give you enough reason to make cupcakes.

Not only that... it's a trip back in time... you can't help but remember your mother, grandmother, aunt or favorite friend who made cupcakes with you. Flour and sugar were everywhere, dirty bowls in the sink, little bottles of food coloring and little boxes of multi-colored sprinkles, confetti and flashy little decorations just waiting to top your cupcakes.

And when you were finished... they were beautiful... every one a masterpiece. Jump right in to your own little fantasyland and make your cupcakes dance around the room.

You can make stars, flowers, cute little critters, ribbons, stripes, shells, hearts, trees and animals, just about anything you can think of. Just let your imagination go wild.

This is your introduction to easy cupcakes and you can do whatever you want.

We listed prepared icing with each cupcake recipe and recipes for delicious homemade frostings and toppings are on pages 144-156. You decide how much time you have.

We also listed a pastry bag coupled with decorating tips, but these are just suggestions. You may use anything you want and still have a great cupcake. Just have fun. Everyone will have fun just eating them.

The Publisher

Dedication

Cookbook Resources' mission is

Bringing Family and Friends to the Table.

We recognize the importance of shared meals as a means of building family bonds with memories and traditions that will last a lifetime. At mealtimes we share more than food. We share ourselves.

This cookbook is dedicated with gratitude and respect to all those who show their love by making home-cooked meals and bringing family and friends to the table.

5

Contents

Continued next page...

Contents

All Day Everyday Cupcakes – continued

Special Occasion Cupcakes

Contents

Frostings, Icings and Toppings

Inspiration, Ideas and Tools

Easy Basic Cupcakes

½ cup shortening
1 cup sugar
3 eggs
1¾ cups flour
2 teaspoons baking powder
½ cup milk
1 teaspoon vanilla

 Preheat oven to 350°.

Cream shortening, sugar and eggs together until light and fluffy. Sift flour, baking powder and ½ teaspoon salt and add alternately with milk to creamed mixture.

Add vanilla. Beat thoroughly. Pour into paper liners in cupcake pans. Bake for 15 to 20 minutes. Yields 18 cupcakes.

Decorations:

1 (12 ounce) container ready-to-serve
        vanilla frosting
1 (10 ounce) container prepared cake icing

 Spread cupcakes with vanilla frosting using icing spatula or back of spoon. Draw your favorite designs on each cupcake using cake icing in a squeezable tube with small nozzle tip.

TIP: Any of the homemade frostings on pages 144-156 will work with these cupcakes.

Vanilla-Cinnamon Cupcakes

2½ cups flour
1 (3.4 ounce) package instant French vanilla
      pudding mix
2 teaspoons ground cinnamon
½ teaspoon baking powder
½ teaspoon baking soda
⅓ cup sugar
3 eggs
1 cup buttermilk*
½ cup canola oil
1 teaspoon vanilla
1 cup miniature semi-sweet chocolate chips

 Preheat oven to 350°.

 Combine flour, pudding mix, cinnamon, baking
powder, baking soda, sugar and a little salt in bowl.

 In separate bowl, combine eggs, buttermilk, oil
and vanilla; mix well and add mixture to dry
ingredients. Whisk for 1 to 2 minutes and fold in
chocolate chips.

Place paper baking cups in 18 muffin cups and fill
with batter about two-thirds full.

Bake for 18 to 21 minutes or until a toothpick
inserted in center comes out clean. Cool for about
5 minutes before removing from pan. Allow
cupcakes to cool completely before frosting. Yields
18 cupcakes.

Continued next page...

Continued from previous page...

Decorations:

**1 (12 ounce) container ready-to-serve
vanilla frosting
1 teaspoon vanilla
Cinnamon**

 Combine frosting and 1 teaspoon vanilla. Spread
frosting over all cupcakes using pastry bag fitted
with large star tip. Sprinkle with cinnamon.

**TIP: To make buttermilk, mix 1 cup milk with
1 tablespoon lemon juice or vinegar and let
milk stand for about 10 minutes.*

Q: How do chickens bake a cake?

A: From scratch.

If cupcakes are still warm, the icing
may soften or melt. Always cool
cupcakes completely before icing.

Double Butterscotch Cupcakes

2 cups flour
1¼ cups sugar
1 (3.4 ounce) package instant butterscotch
       pudding mix
1 (3.4 ounce) package instant vanilla
       pudding mix
2 teaspoons baking powder
4 eggs, lightly beaten
¾ cup canola oil
1 teaspoon vanilla
1 (12 ounce) package butterscotch chips

 Preheat oven to 350°.

 Place paper baking cups in 24 muffin cups.
Combine flour, sugar, both pudding mixes, baking
powder and ½ teaspoon salt in bowl.

In separate bowl, combine 1 cup water, eggs, oil
and vanilla; stir this mixture into dry ingredients
and mix just until moist. Stir in 1 cup butterscotch
chips and mix well.

 Spoon batter into muffin cups about two-thirds
full. Bake for 16 to 20 minutes or until toothpick
inserted in center comes out clean. Cool for
5 minutes before removing from pan. Cool
completely before frosting. Yields 24 cupcakes.

Continued next page...

Continued from previous page...

Decorations:

**1 (12 ounce) container ready-to-serve
                buttercream frosting**
1 (8 ounce) package toffee bits

 Use a pastry bag fitted with a star tip number
28 or 30, depending on the size you want. Squeeze
bag evenly around cupcake from outside to inside.
Sprinkle toffee on top.

Use a pastry bag fitted with a star tip number
28 or 30, depending on the size you want. Squeeze
bag evenly around cupcake from outside to inside.
Sprinkle toffee on top.

If you wanted a little different twist for the
frosting, coconut-pecan frosting is great on these
cupcakes.

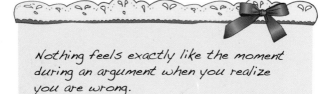

*Nothing feels exactly like the moment
during an argument when you realize
you are wrong.*

*To create a smooth finish, dip the
spatula or knife in hot water after
frosting the cupcakes and gently
smooth the surface of the frosting.*

Double Butterscotch Cupcakes ▶

Sour Cream Cupcakes

1 tablespoon shortening
1 cup sugar
2 eggs
½ teaspoon baking soda
½ cup sour cream
1½ cups flour
½ teaspoon cream of tartar
⅛ teaspoon mace

 Preheat oven to 350°.

 Cream shortening, sugar and eggs together until light and fluffy. Dissolve baking soda in sour cream.

 Sift flour, 1½ teaspoons salt, cream of tartar and mace together and add alternately with sour cream to first mixture. Beat thoroughly.

Bake in sprayed or paper-lined cupcake pans for 18 to 22 minutes. Yields 18 cupcakes.

Decorations:

1 (12 ounce) container ready-to-serve
        vanilla frosting
1 fresh orange
Sugar

Spread frosting over top of cupcakes using an icing spatula or back of a spoon. Carefully cut strips of orange peel (do not get any white pith) and roll in a little sugar. Arrange orange strips (zest) on top of cupcakes.

White Velvet Cupcakes

1 (18 ounce) box white cake mix
⅓ cup canola oil
1 teaspoon almond extract
3 large egg whites
1 cup white chocolate chips

 Preheat oven to 350°.

 Place paper baking cups in 24 muffin cups. Beat cake mix, 1¼ cups water, oil, almond extract and egg whites in bowl on low speed for 30 seconds.

 Increase speed to medium and beat for 2 minutes. Stir in white chocolate chips. Divide batter among muffin cups.

Bake for 19 to 22 minutes or until toothpick inserted in center comes out clean. Cool for 10 minutes before removing from pan. Cool for 30 minutes before frosting. Yields 24 cupcakes.

Decorations:

1 (16 ounce) container ready-to-serve classic
 white frosting
1 (2 ounce) bottle red or pink sanding sugar
 or sprinkles

Use a pastry bag fitted with a closed star tip number 28 or 30, depending on the size you want. Squeeze bag evenly around cupcake from outside to inside. Scatter colored sanding sugar or sprinkles on top.

Surprise Cupcakes

1 (8 ounce) package cream cheese, softened
2 cups sugar, divided
1 egg, slightly beaten
1 cup white chocolate chips
1½ cups flour
1 teaspoon baking soda
⅓ cup canola oil

 Preheat oven to 350°.

 Place paper baking cups in 18 muffin cups. Combine cream cheese, ½ cup sugar, oil and egg in bowl and beat until mixture is smooth; stir in white chocolate chips.

 In separate bowl, combine remaining 1½ cups sugar, flour, baking soda, oil and 1 cup water and mix well, but not too vigorously.

 Fill muffin cups one-third full with batter and place 1 heaping tablespoon cream cheese mixture over each cupcake. (You may need to add a little to each cupcake to use up all the cream cheese mixture.)

 Bake for 20 to 24 minutes or until toothpick inserted in center comes out clean. Cool on wire rack. Remove cupcakes from pan and cool completely before storing. Yields 18 cupcakes.

Decorations:

Powdered sugar
Fresh fruit

 Frost these cupcakes with a heavy dusting of powdered sugar and top with fresh fruit. Raspberries are great with white chocolate!

White and Dark Chocolate Cupcakes

1 (18 ounce) box French vanilla cake mix
⅓ cup canola oil
3 eggs
1 teaspoon vanilla
1 cup white chocolate chips
    or 1 cup dark chocolate chips
    or ½ cup white chocolate and ½ cup dark
        chocolate chips

 Preheat oven to 350°.

 Place paper baking cups in 24 muffin cups. Combine cake mix, 1¼ cups water, oil, eggs and vanilla in bowl and beat on low for 30 seconds.

 Increase speed to medium and beat for 2 minutes. Stir in white chocolate chips. Spoon evenly into muffin cups.

 Bake for 18 to 23 minutes or until toothpick inserted in center comes out clean.

Cool for 5 minutes before removing from pan. Cool for 30 minutes before frosting. Yields 24 cupcakes.

Decorations:

1 (16 ounce) container ready-to-serve
    white frosting
24 edible sugar flowers

 Use a pastry bag fitted with a star tip number 35 or 54, depending on the size you want.

Continued next page...

Continued from previous page...

 Squeeze bag evenly around cupcake from outside to inside.

 Place edible sugar flower and leaf on top. An advanced class in decorating teaches how to make flowers and leaves.

TIP: Instead of the flowers, you can always use a Hershey® bar and a potato peeler to make some chocolate curls.

The U.S. produces more chocolate than any other country but the Swiss consume the most per capita, followed closely by the English.

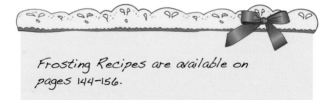

Frosting Recipes are available on pages 144-156.

Granola-Chocolate Chip Cupcakes

1 cup granola cereal
1⅓ cups flour
½ cup sugar
2 teaspoons baking powder
¾ teaspoon baking soda
2 eggs, beaten
1 (8 ounce) carton plain yogurt
⅓ cup canola oil
½ teaspoon vanilla
½ cup chopped pecans
1 cup chocolate chips

Preheat oven to 350°.

Place paper baking cups in 24 muffin cups. Combine cereal, flour, sugar, baking powder, baking soda and a pinch of salt in large bowl.

In smaller bowl, combine eggs, yogurt, oil and vanilla and stir into dry ingredients just until moist. Stir in pecans and chocolate chips.

Fill muffin cups three-fourths full with batter and bake for 13 to 15 minutes or until toothpick inserted in center comes out clean.

Cool in pan for about 5 minutes. Remove from pan and cool completely before frosting. Yields 12 cupcakes.

Continued next page...

Continued from previous page...

Decorations:

1 (16 ounce) ready-to-serve milk chocolate frosting, optional
or
¾ cup chopped nuts, toasted

 These are delicious as is, but if you want a topping one of these suggestions will be terrific. To toast nuts, spread out on baking sheet and bake at 250° for 10 to 15 minutes. Toasting brings out the flavor in nuts.

Cupcakes probably got their name because they were baked in small cups for faster baking and the ingredients were measured in cups rather than by pounds.

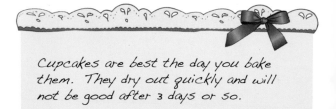

Cupcakes are best the day you bake them. They dry out quickly and will not be good after 3 days or so.

Granola-Chocolate Chip Cupcakes ▶

Chocolate Chip Cupcakes

1 (18 ounce) box yellow cake mix
3 eggs
⅓ cup canola oil
1 teaspoon vanilla
1 (12 ounce) package chocolate chips
1 cup chopped pecans, optional

 Preheat oven to 350°.

 Place paper baking cups in 24 muffin cups. Combine cake mix, 1¼ cups water, eggs, oil and vanilla in bowl.

 Beat on low speed for 30 seconds, increase speed to medium and beat for 2 minutes. Fold in chocolate chips and pecans and spoon batter into muffin cups.

Bake for 19 to 22 minutes or until toothpick inserted in center comes out clean. Cool for 5 to 10 minutes in pan. Remove from pan and place cupcakes on wire rack to cool completely before frosting. Yields 24 cupcakes.

Decorations:

These cupcakes do not really need a frosting, but if you want that "sugar splurge", a chocolate frosting would do well. You could call it Double-Chocolate, Chocolate Chip!

Harvest Pumpkin Cupcakes

1 (15 ounce) can pumpkin
3 eggs, slightly beaten
½ cup oil
1½ teaspoons ground cinnamon
1 teaspoon baking soda
1 (18 ounce) box yellow cake mix
½ cup chopped walnuts

 Preheat oven to 350°.

 Place paper baking cups in 24 muffin cups. Combine pumpkin, eggs, oil, cinnamon and baking soda in bowl and mix well.

 Add cake mix, ¼ cup water and beat for 1 minute on low speed. Increase speed to high and beat for 2 minutes. Fold in walnuts.

 Fill muffin cups two-thirds full and bake for 19 to 22 minutes or until toothpick inserted in center comes out clean. Cool for 10 minutes in pan; remove from pan and cool completely before frosting. Yields 24 cupcakes.

Decorations:

1 (16 ounce) container ready-to-serve
        buttercream frosting
1 (2 ounce) bottle yellow, brown and
        orange sprinkles

 Spread frosting in swirling motion over cupcakes and top with sprinkles.

 If you like, use 1 (2 ounce) bottle sugar-cinnamon gems instead of sprinklers. The cinnamon gems really complement the pumpkin in the cupcakes.

Spicy Cupcakes

½ cup shortening
1 cup sugar
2 egg yolks
⅓ cup chopped raisins
⅓ cup chopped walnuts
1 teaspoon baking soda
2½ cups flour
½ teaspoon ground cloves
½ teaspoon ground mace
1½ teaspoons ground cinnamon
¾ cup buttermilk*
1 egg white, stiffly beaten

 Preheat oven to 350°.

 Cream shortening, sugar and egg yolks in mixing bowl. Add raisins and walnuts. Dissolve baking soda in 1 tablespoon hot water and add to mixture.

 Mix and sift flour, ½ teaspoon salt and spices and add alternately with buttermilk to first mixture. Fold in one stiffly beaten egg white.

 Turn in sprayed or paper-lined muffin cups and bake for 15 to 20 minutes. Yields 18 cupcakes.

Decorations:

Ready-to-serve cream cheese frosting
18 walnut halves

 Use a pastry bag fitted with a ruffle tip number 86 or 100, depending on the size you want.

Continued next page...

Continued from previous page...

Squeeze bag evenly around cupcake from outside to inside. If you don't have these tips, try a star tip. Top with walnut halves.

TIP: To make buttermilk, mix 1 cup milk with 1 tablespoon lemon juice or vinegar and let milk stand for about 10 minutes.

Cupcakes are called "Fairy Cakes" in the United Kingdom.

If you are baking in a pan with a dark or non-stick surface, you should lower the recommended recipe temperature by 25° to avoid overbrowning. Dark pans give your cakes a darker finish when baked at 350°.

Maple-Cream Cupcakes

1½ cups flour
⅓ cup sugar
3 teaspoons baking powder
1 teaspoon ground cinnamon
1 teaspoon ground nutmeg
¼ cup shortening
¾ cup quick-cooking oats
1 egg, beaten
½ cup milk
½ cup maple syrup

 Preheat oven to 350°.

 Place paper baking cups in 16 muffin cups. Sift flour, sugar, baking powder, ¼ teaspoon salt, cinnamon and nutmeg in bowl. Cut in shortening until mixture resembles coarse crumbs.

 Stir in oats; add egg, milk and maple syrup; stir only until dry ingredients are moist. Fill muffin cups one-half full.

 Bake for 18 to 21 minutes. Let stand in pan for about 5 minutes. Cool completely before frosting. Yields 16 cupcakes.

Decorations:

1 (12 ounce) container ready-to-serve
        buttercream frosting
2 tablespoons maple syrup
1 tablespoon butter, melted
Ground cinnamon

 Place buttercream frosting in small bowl, stir in maple syrup and melted butter; blend well.

Continued next page...

Continued from previous page...

 Use a pastry bag fitted with a round tip number 10 to 12, depending on the size you want. Start in the middle, squeeze bag evenly and slowly pull straight up.

Sprinkle frosting with cinnamon. Coconut-pecan frosting with a sprinkling of finely chopped pecans would also be great with these.

There are many different sizes and shapes of tips coupled to pastry bags to create designs with frosting. The suggested tip number written in "Decorations" for each recipe may be changed without affecting the taste of the cupcake.

If you don't have a pastry bag or a certain decorating tip, substitute a small plastic bag. Fill bag half way with frosting, cut a small hole in one bottom corner, and squeeze onto cupcake.

Creamy Apple Cupcakes

1 (3 ounce) package cream cheese, softened
1 cup sugar
2 eggs
½ cup milk
¼ cup (½ stick) butter, melted
1 tablespoon lemon juice
1 teaspoon vanilla
1½ cups flour
1½ teaspoons baking powder
½ teaspoon baking soda
1 tart apple, peeled, diced
½ cup bran flakes

 Preheat oven to 350°.

 Place paper baking cups in 14 muffin cups.
Combine cream cheese, sugar, eggs, milk,
butter, lemon juice and vanilla in bowl and
beat until smooth.

 In separate bowl, combine flour, baking powder,
baking soda and ¼ teaspoon salt and stir into
cream cheese mixture just until moist. Fold in
diced apples and bran flakes.

 Spread batter into muffin cups two-thirds full.
Bake for 21 to 25 minutes or until toothpick
inserted in center comes out clean. Cool in pan
for about 5 minutes.

Remove to wire rack to cool completely.
These cupcakes need to be refrigerated.
Yields 14 cupcakes.

Continued next page...

Continued from previous page...

Decorations:

**1 (12 ounce) container ready-to-serve cream
cheese frosting**
4 walnuts, shelled, quartered

 Use a pastry bag fitted with an open star tip
number 17 or 21, depending on the size you want.
Squeeze bag evenly in four sections to make wings
of butterfly. Put a walnut quarter on top.

*TIP: Dutch Apple-Nut Crumble Topping on page 155 is a
great topping to change up this recipe and it's so easy.*

*When using foil cups, remove paper
inserts, if included, before filling and
baking; inserts are included to help
separate the thin foil cups.*

*Why did the little cupcake major in
hotel and restaurant management?*

Because it wanted to be a hostess.

Sweet Banana-Strawberry Cupcakes

½ cup (1 stick) butter, softened
½ cup sugar
⅓ cup packed brown sugar
2 large ripe bananas, mashed
2 large eggs
1 teaspoon vanilla
2¼ cups flour
2 teaspoons baking powder
½ teaspoon baking soda
½ cup buttermilk*
½ cup strawberry preserves
1 cup milk chocolate chips

 Preheat oven to 350°.

 Place paper baking cups in 18 muffin cups. Beat butter, sugar and brown sugar in bowl until light and fluffy. Beat in bananas, eggs and vanilla.

 In separate bowl, combine flour, baking powder, baking soda and a pinch of salt. Alternately add one-third flour mixture and half of buttermilk to butter mixture and end with flour mixture. Stir in strawberry preserves and chocolate chips.

Divide batter evenly among muffin cups and bake for 21 to 25 minutes or until toothpick inserted in center comes out clean. Cool in pan for about 5 minutes. Cool completely before frosting. Yields 18 cupcakes.

Continued next page...

Continued from previous page...

Decorations:

**1 (16 ounce) container ready-to-serve
            strawberry frosting**
Nonpareils

Use a pastry bag fitted with an open star tip
number 17 or 21, depending on the size you want.
Squeeze bag evenly around cupcake from outside
to inside. Scatter nonpareils or sprinkles on top.

**TIP: To make buttermilk, mix 1 cup milk with 1 tablespoon
        lemon juice or vinegar and let milk stand for about
        10 minutes.*

To avoid crumbs in frosting, dust the
top of cupcakes with your finger to
remove loose crumbs. Spread a thin
layer of frosting before putting the
final layer of frosting down to avoid
crumbs resurfacing. Wash knife with
hot water when too much frosting
sticks to it.

Sweet Banana-Strawberry Cupcakes ▶

Banana-Nut Cupcakes

1 (18 ounce) box banana nut cake mix
⅔ cup milk
2 tablespoons canola oil
1 egg

 Preheat oven to 350°.

Place paper baking cups in 12 muffin cups.
Combine cake mix, milk, oil and egg in medium
bowl. Stir mixture just until it blends well. (Batter
will be slightly lumpy.)

Divide batter among muffin cups and sprinkle
walnuts from cake mix evenly over batter.

Bake for about 20 minutes or until golden brown
and tops spring back when touched. Cool in pan
for 10 minutes; cool completely before frosting.
Yields 12 cupcakes.

Decorations:

1 (12 ounce) container ready-to-serve
        buttercream frosting
1 (2 ounce) bottle pastel sprinkles

 Use a pastry bag fitted with an open star tip
number 17 or 19, depending on the size you want.
Squeeze bag evenly around cupcake from outside
to inside. Top with sprinkles

*What was Snow White's brother's
name? Egg White! Get the yoke?*

Banana-Chocolate Chip Cupcakes

½ cup (1 stick) butter, softened
⅔ cup sugar
½ cup packed brown sugar
2 eggs
1½ cups (about 3) mashed ripe bananas
3 teaspoons vanilla
2 cups flour
3 teaspoons baking soda
1 cup chopped pecans
1 (6 ounce) package milk chocolate chips

 Preheat oven to 350°.

Place paper baking cups in 24 muffin cups. Cream butter, sugar and brown sugar in bowl until smooth. Beat in eggs, bananas and vanilla.

 In separate bowl, combine flour and baking soda and add to creamed mixture just until it blends well. Stir in pecans and chocolate chips and fill muffin cups half full.

 Bake for 16 to 20 minutes or until a toothpick inserted in center comes out clean. Cool for 5 minutes before removing from pan. Cool completely before frosting. Yields 24 cupcakes.

Decorations:

1 (16 ounce) container ready-to-serve
          buttercream frosting
1½ cups mini chocolate chips
24 mini chocolate chip cookies, optional

 Use a pastry bag fitted with an open star tip number 17 or 21, depending on the size you want.

Continued next page...

Continued from previous page...

 Squeeze bag evenly around cupcake from outside to inside, but let the cupcake show.

 Sprinkle mini chocolate chips over frosting. Place a mini chocolate chip cookie in frosting.

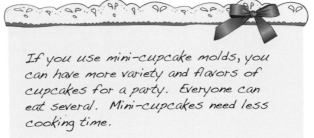

If you use mini-cupcake molds, you can have more variety and flavors of cupcakes for a party. Everyone can eat several. Mini-cupcakes need less cooking time.

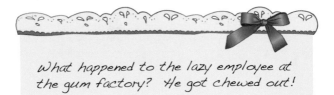

What happened to the lazy employee at the gum factory? He got chewed out!

Blueberry-Spice Cupcakes

¾ cup sugar
½ cup (1 stick) butter, softened
1¾ cups plus 1 tablespoon flour
2½ teaspoons baking powder
¾ teaspoon ground cinnamon
¼ teaspoon ground nutmeg
1 egg, lightly beaten
¾ cup milk
1½ cups fresh blueberries

 Preheat oven to 350°.

 Place paper baking cups in 12 muffin cups.
Cream sugar and butter. In separate bowl,
combine flour, baking powder, cinnamon,
nutmeg and ¼ teaspoon salt.

Add egg and milk to sugar-butter mixture and
stir in dry ingredients just until moist. Gently fold
in blueberries.

Spoon batter into muffin cups about two-thirds
full. Bake for 17 to 21 minutes or until toothpick
inserted in center comes out clean. Cool for
5 minutes before removing from pan. Let
cupcakes completely cool before frosting.
Yields 12 cupcakes.

Continued next page...

Continued from previous page...

Decorations:

1 (12 ounce) container ready-to-serve
       white frosting
White fondant
Edible flowers or chocolate bar, optional

 Spread a thin coat of frosting over top of cupcake to keep crumbs out of fondant. Lay white fondant on top and trim around liner.

 Top with edible sugar flowers or paint your own with tube of decorating gel.

 If you don't have any decoration for the cupcake, put some blueberries on top.

TIP: For a quick cupcake decoration, hold a chocolate bar on its side and use a potato peeler to make chocolate curls.

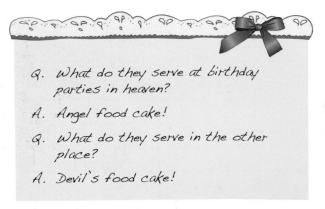

Q. What do they serve at birthday parties in heaven?

A. Angel food cake!

Q. What do they serve in the other place?

A. Devil's food cake!

Blueberry-Spice Cupcakes ▶

Cherry-Honey Cupcakes

1½ cups quick-cooking oats
1 cup flour
⅓ cup packed brown sugar
3 teaspoons baking powder
1 egg
⅔ cup milk
⅓ cup canola oil
⅓ cup honey
18 to 24 fresh sweet cherries, coarsely chopped

 Preheat oven to 350°.

 Place paper baking cups in 18 muffin cups. Combine oats, flour, brown sugar, baking powder and a pinch of salt in large bowl.

 In separate bowl, combine egg, milk, oil and honey and stir into dry ingredients just until moist. Stir in cherries and pour into muffin cups, about two-thirds full.

 Bake for 16 to 18 minutes or until toothpick inserted in center comes out clean. Let stand in pan for about 5 minutes. Let cool completely before frosting. Yields 18 cupcakes.

Decorations:

1 (12 ounce) container vanilla frosting
18 maraschino cherries

Use a pastry bag fitted with an open star tip number 17 or 21 or closed star tip number 30 or 35. Squeeze bag evenly around cupcake from outside to inside, but let some of the cupcake show. Top with cherry.

Continued next page...

Continued from previous page...

A 2-quart plastic freezer bag is a good substitute for a pastry bag. Fill bag about one-third full and cut a small slit in the bottom corner of one side. Squeeze frosting out of bag to check the size of the hole. If you want a wider line of frosting, enlarge the hole.

Dip your knife in cold water several times while you are frosting cupcakes or a cake. It will keep the excess frosting from drying out on the knife.

Expert bakers say to bring all ingredients to room temperature before mixing to promote a creamy texture and to minimize lumps and graininess.

Carrot Cake Cupcakes

1 (18 ounce) box carrot cake mix
3 eggs
½ cup canola oil
1 (8 ounce) can crushed pineapple with juice
¾ cup chopped pecans

 Preheat oven to 350°.

 Place paper baking cups in 24 muffin cups. Mix cake mix, eggs, oil, pineapple and ½ cup water in bowl and beat on low speed for 1 minute.

 Increase speed to medium and beat for 2 minutes. Fold in pecans and spoon into muffin cups.

Bake for 19 to 23 minutes or until toothpick inserted in center comes out clean. Cool in pan for 5 minutes. Remove cupcakes from pan and cool completely before frosting. Yields 24 cupcakes.

Decorations:

1 (16 ounce) container ready-to-serve cream
            cheese frosting
Food coloring
24 sugar or fondant carrots, optional
Powdered sugar, optional
Pecan pieces, optional

Use a pastry bag fitted with a round tip number 5. It's good for thin lines, writing and dots. Tips 2, 3, 4 have smaller holes and will make finer lines, but they may be too small for some icings.

Continued next page...

Continued from previous page...

 Add food coloring to remaining frosting as needed. Make a carrot with a large round tip number 2A or 1A. The carrot stem needs an open star tip about number 15.

 The easiest topping for these cupcakes is to sprinkle powdered sugar and pecan pieces over the top.

TIP: To make your own pastry bag, see page 157.

February 3: National Carrot Cake Day

Q. What type of cupcakes do horses like?

A. Carrot cake cupcakes!

Small muffin-shaped cakes were first made because it took so long to bake a cake in a hearth oven.

Carrot Cake Cupcakes ▶

Fresh Lemon Cupcakes

1 (18 ounce) box lemon cake mix
⅓ cup canola oil
3 eggs
1 (8 ounce) can crushed pineapple, drained

 Preheat oven to 350°.

Place paper baking cups in 24 muffin cups.
Combine cake mix, 1¼ cups water, oil and eggs
in bowl and beat on low speed for 30 seconds.
Increase mixer speed to medium and beat for
2 minutes. Stir in pineapple and mix well.

Spoon into muffin cups and bake for 18 to
22 minutes or until toothpick inserted in center
comes out clean. Cool in pan for about 5 minutes.
Cool to room temperature before frosting. Yields
24 cupcakes.

Decorations:

1 (16 ounce) container ready-to-serve
            lemon frosting
2 - 3 lemons, thinly sliced

Use a pastry bag fitted with a closed star tip
number 30 or 31, depending on the size you want.
Drop individual flowers over cupcakes; top with
thin half slice of lemon.

All cupcakes do not have to be round.
There are cupcake molds in the shape
of stars, hearts, flowers, etc.

Sweet Orange Cupcakes

½ cup (1 stick) unsalted butter, softened
1¼ cups sugar
2 large eggs
1 (8 ounce) carton plain yogurt
2 cups flour
1 teaspoon baking soda
½ cup chopped pecans
½ cup orange marmalade
1 teaspoon orange extract

 Preheat oven to 350°.

 Cream butter and sugar in bowl. Beat in eggs and yogurt for 1 minute. Add flour and baking soda and stir into creamed mixture; stir just until mixture is moist. Fold in pecans, orange marmalade and orange extract.

 Place paper baking cups in 18 muffin cups and fill muffin cups three-fourths full. Bake for 18 to 21 minutes or until toothpick inserted in center comes out clean.

Cool in pan for about 5 minutes. Remove from pan and cool completely before frosting. Yields 18 cupcakes.

Decorations:

1 (16 ounce) container ready-to-serve cream
        cheese frosting
Orange sanding sugar
Fresh orange slices

 Use a pastry bag fitted with a round tip between number 10 or 12, depending on the size you want. Start on the outside, slowly squeeze and pull straight up when finished.

Continued next page...

Continued from previous page...

 Top with sanding sugar and garnish with fresh
orange slices.

 If you want a flavored orange icing, stir ½ cup
orange marmalade or 1 tablespoon thawed
orange juice concentrate into frosting.

The toothpick test is a great way to
test cupcakes to know when they
are done. Insert a toothpick into
the center of the cupcake. If it
comes out clean, it is done. If it
has cake stuck to it, it needs to cook
a little longer.

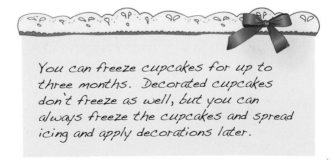

You can freeze cupcakes for up to
three months. Decorated cupcakes
don't freeze as well, but you can
always freeze the cupcakes and spread
icing and apply decorations later.

Raspberry-Filled Lemon Cupcakes

2 cups flour
2½ teaspoons baking powder
¼ teaspoon baking soda
¾ cup (1½ sticks) unsalted butter, softened
1¼ cups sugar
1 egg plus 3 egg yolks
1 tablespoon lemon juice, plus enough milk to
        equal ¾ cup
1 tablespoon grated lemon peel
½ cup seedless raspberry jam

 Preheat oven to 350°.

 Place paper baking cups in 16 muffin cups. Sift
flour, baking powder, baking soda and ¼ teaspoon
salt in bowl.

In separate bowl, beat butter and sugar until
mixture lightens. Beat in egg and egg yolks and
mix well. Add flour mixture alternating with
lemon juice-milk mixture, beginning and ending
with flour. Stir in lemon peel.

 Spoon heaping ¼ cup batter into each liner
and bake for 20 to 23 minutes or until toothpick
inserted in center comes out clean. Remove from
pan and cool completely on rack before frosting.

Poke a hole in center of each cupcake with handle
of wooden spoon. Go almost to the bottom while
cupcakes are still hot.

Continued next page...

Continued from previous page...

Place raspberry jam in plastic bag and snip off a small corner. Dip corner of bag into hole and pipe about 1½ teaspoons jam into center of each cupcake. Yields 16 cupcakes.

Decorations:

1 (12 ounce) container ready-to-serve white frosting
1 pint fresh raspberries

Spread frosting over top of cupcakes using an icing spatula or back of spoon. Top with fresh raspberries. Lemon icing is also amazing!

Fillings in cupcakes are an added surprise to any bite. Use a decorating bag to inject icings, custards and cremes into the center of cupcakes or dig out a small hole, fill with cremes, etc. and replace a piece of cake in the hole.

Raspberry-Filled Lemon Cupcakes ▶

Tempting Berry Cupcakes

¾ cup fresh blueberries
¾ cup coarsely chopped fresh strawberries
1 cup sugar, divided
1 (8 ounce) package cream cheese, softened
2 eggs
1 teaspoon vanilla
1¼ cups flour
1 teaspoon baking soda

 Preheat oven to 350°.

 Place paper baking cups in 12 muffin cups. Combine blueberries, strawberries and ¼ cup sugar in bowl and set aside.

 In separate bowl, beat cream cheese and remaining sugar until mixture is smooth. Add eggs one at a time and beat well after each addition; stir in vanilla.

 Combine flour, baking soda and pinch of salt in bowl and stir into creamed mixture. Fold in berries and fill muffin cups two-thirds full.

 Bake for 18 to 21 minutes or until toothpick inserted in center comes out clean. Cool for about 5 minutes before removing from pan.

 Cool completely on wire rack before frosting. These cupcakes need to be refrigerated. Yields 12 cupcakes.

Continued next page...

Continued from previous page...

Decorations:

**1 (12 ounce) container ready-to-serve cream
cheese frosting**
1 pint fresh strawberries, sliced to stem

 Use a pastry bag fitted with an open star tip
number 17 or 21 to place a thick layer of cream
cheese frosting over cupcakes. Place strawberries
on top of frosting.

Using frozen berries for cupcakes instead of fresh
berries makes cupcakes heavier because they have
much more liquid than fresh berries.

*If you are out of toothpicks to test
cupcakes to see if they are done, use
the touch method. Lightly touch the
top of the cupcake. If it springs
back, it is done. If it does not spring
back, it needs to cook a little longer.*

*Some mistakes are too much fun to
only make once.*

Creamy Strawberry Cupcakes

1 (18 ounce) box super-moist yellow cake mix
1 (8 ounce) carton sour cream
½ cup canola oil
2 eggs
¼ cup strawberry preserves at room temperature
1 (3 ounce) package cream cheese, cut into
   24 pieces

 Preheat oven to 350°.

 Place paper baking cups in 24 muffin cups.
Combine cake mix, sour cream, oil, ½ cup water
and eggs in large bowl with spoon until they blend
well. (Batter will be thick.) Divide batter evenly
among muffin cups.

 In separate bowl, stir strawberry preserves until
smooth. Place 1 piece cream cheese on top of
batter in each cupcake and press down slightly.
Place ¼ teaspoon preserves over cream cheese.

Bake for 18 to 23 minutes or until tops are golden
brown and toothpick inserted in center comes
out clean. Cool for 10 minutes before removing
from pan. Cool completely before frosting.
These cupcakes need to be refrigerated. Yields
24 cupcakes.

Continued next page...

February 27: National Strawberry Day

Continued from previous page...

Decorations:

1 (16 ounce) container ready-to-serve
            strawberry frosting
1 (3 ounce) bottle nonpareils or sprinkles

Use a pastry bag fitted with an open star tip
number 16 or 18, depending on the size you want.
Squeeze bag evenly around cupcake from outside
to inside, but let some of the cupcake show. Drop
sprinkles or nonpareils on top.

Because the ingredients were expensive,
cake itself was considered to be a rich
man's food in early America. After the
American Industrial Revolution took
place between 1780 and 1860, baking
ingredients were easier to come by and
more affordable for common folk.

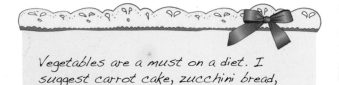

Vegetables are a must on a diet. I
suggest carrot cake, zucchini bread,
and pumpkin pie. *Jim Davis, Garfield*

Creamy Strawberry Cupcakes ▶

Strawberry Delight

1 (18 ounce) box strawberry cake mix
3 eggs
⅓ cup canola oil
1 (6 ounce) package white chocolate chips

 Preheat oven to 350°.

 Place paper baking cups in 24 muffin cups.
Combine cake mix, eggs, oil and 1¼ cups water in
bowl and beat on low speed for about 30 seconds.

 Increase speed to medium and beat for 2 minutes.
Stir in white chocolate chips and spoon about
¼ cup batter into each muffin cup.

 Bake for 19 to 23 minutes or until toothpick
inserted in center comes out clean. Cool in pan for
5 to 10 minutes. Cool completely before frosting.
Yields 24 cupcakes.

Decorations:

1 (16 ounce) container ready-to-serve
            strawberry frosting
1 (2 ounce) bottle multi-colored sprinkles

Use a pastry bag fitted with an open star tip
number 21. Squeeze bag evenly around
cupcake from outside to inside. Top with
multi-colored sprinkles.

TIP: If you can't find the right color frosting for your
    cupcakes, don't hesitate to use food coloring. Just
    remember, a little can be a lot of color.

Poppy Seed-Strawberry Cupcakes

2 cups flour
¾ cup sugar
1 tablespoon baking powder
1 tablespoon poppy seeds
½ teaspoon ground cinnamon
1 egg
¾ cup milk
¼ cup (½ stick) unsalted butter, melted
½ cup strawberry preserves

 Preheat oven to 350°.

Place paper baking cups in 16 muffin cups. Combine flour, sugar, baking powder, poppy seeds and cinnamon in bowl.

 In separate bowl, beat egg, milk and butter and stir into dry ingredients just until moist. Fold in strawberry preserves and mix well. Fill muffin cups with batter two-thirds full.

Bake for 19 to 23 minutes or until toothpick inserted in center comes out clean and muffins are golden brown.

 Cool for at least 5 minutes before removing from pan. Cool completely before frosting. Yields 16 cupcakes.

Decorations:

1 (12 ounce) container ready-to-serve
        vanilla frosting
1 pint fresh strawberries, halved

 Spread frosting over cupcakes with icing spatula or back of spoon. Top with strawberry half.

Zucchini Cupcakes

*These are not too sweet – just right for a
quick, healthy lunch box or snack treat.*

1½ cups self-rising flour
1 teaspoon baking soda
1½ teaspoons pumpkin pie spice
3 egg whites or ¾ cup egg substitute
¾ cup packed brown sugar
½ cup canola oil
2 cups peeled, grated zucchini

 Preheat oven to 350°.

 Combine flour, baking soda and pumpkin pie
spice in small bowl.

 Beat eggs, brown sugar and oil in mixing bowl
for about 3 minutes. Add zucchini and stir until
they blend well. Add flour mixture and stir until
ingredients combine thoroughly.

 Fill paper-lined muffin cups three-fourths full and
bake for 20 to 25 minutes. Cool pan on wire rack
5 minutes; let cupcakes cool completely before
frosting. Yields 12 cupcakes.

Decorations:

Cream cheese frosting, optional
1½ cups walnut pieces, optional

These are delicious without a frosting, but if you
want a frosting, cream cheese is delicious with
these cupcakes. Frost each cupcake and top with
walnut pieces.

Brunch-Time Cupcakes

2½ cups flour
1½ cups sugar
2 teaspoons ground cinnamon
2 teaspoons baking soda
3 eggs, lightly beaten
¾ cup applesauce
½ cup canola oil
1 teaspoon vanilla
1½ cups dried cranberries or Craisins®
1 tart apple, peeled, grated
1 (8 ounce) can crushed pineapple, drained
½ cup flaked coconut
¾ cup chopped pecans

 Preheat oven to 350°.

 Place paper baking cups in 24 muffin cups.
Combine flour, sugar, cinnamon, baking soda
and ½ teaspoon salt in bowl. In separate bowl,
combine eggs, applesauce, oil and vanilla.

 Stir mixture into dry ingredients just until moist.
(Batter will be thick.) Stir in cranberries, apple,
pineapple, coconut and pecans.

Spoon batter into muffin cups about two-thirds full
and bake for 21 to 24 minutes or until toothpick
inserted in center comes out clean. Cool in pan
for about 5 minutes and cool completely before
storing. Yields 24 cupcakes.

Decorations:

 These cupcakes are so moist and filled with fruit
goodies that they really don't need frosting.

Tropical Coconut Cupcakes

1 (3 ounce) package cream cheese, softened
1⅓ cups sugar
1 teaspoon vanilla
½ teaspoon almond extract
1 egg
2 cups flour
1 teaspoon baking soda
¼ cup sour cream
1 (15 ounce) can crushed pineapple, drained
⅓ cup chopped, slivered almonds
½ cup flaked coconut

 Preheat oven to 350°.

 Place paper baking cups in 18 muffin cups. Beat cream cheese, sugar, vanilla and almond extract in bowl until smooth and creamy. Stir in egg and mix well.

 In separate bowl, combine flour and baking soda and add to creamed mixture alternately with sour cream, just until moist. Fold in pineapple, almonds and coconut.

 Fill muffin cups three-fourths full. Bake for 24 to 26 minutes or until toothpick inserted in center comes out clean.

Cool in pan for about 10 minutes. Cool completely before frosting. These cupcakes need to be refrigerated. Yields 18 cupcakes.

Continued next page...

Continued from previous page...

Decorations:

White frosting
Yellow food coloring
Powdered sugar

 Mix a few drops of food coloring with frosting. Use a pastry bag fitted with an open star tip number 30 or 54. Squeeze bag evenly around cupcake from outside to inside.

 Pop in oven broiler for a few seconds until the top is a little brown. Dust with powdered sugar.

Q. What cake do bats like?

A. Upside down cake.

Cooking times and the number each recipe makes will vary based on the muffin pan used, how much batter is in each cup, addition of nuts, raisins, etc., and of course, altitude. Keep in mind that the smaller the cupcake, the quicker it cooks. The longer it cooks, the drier it will be.

Coconut Delight Cupcakes

1 cup flour
2 teaspoons baking powder
¾ cup butter-flavored shortening
½ cup (1 stick) butter, softened
1¼ cups sugar
4 egg whites
¾ cup half-and-half cream
1 teaspoon coconut extract
1 cup flaked coconut

 Preheat oven to 350°.

 Place paper baking cups in 14 muffin cups.
Combine flour, baking powder and ½ teaspoon
salt in bowl.

 In separate bowl, beat shortening, butter and
sugar until creamy. Add egg whites and beat until
very light and foamy, about 3 minutes.

Add flour mixture, alternating with half-and-half
cream, beginning and ending with flour mixture.
Stir in coconut extract and coconut. Spoon scant
⅓ cup batter into each cupcake liner.

 Bake for 24 to 27 minutes or until toothpick
inserted in center comes out clean. Remove
from pan and cool completely before frosting.
Yields 14 cupcakes.

Continued next page...

Continued from previous page...

Decorations:

1 (16 ounce) container ready-to-serve buttercream frosting
Yellow food coloring
Edible sugar flowers, optional

 Place buttercream in bowl. Add food coloring until frosting reaches desired color. Use a pastry bag fitted with closed star tip number 30. Squeeze bag evenly around cupcake from outside to inside.

 Place flower on top. If you don't have flowers handy, sprinkle finely grated lemon peel over top.

Teacake is a generic term for cookies, breads, muffins or cakes. People ate them while " taking tea" in an age when people had time to "take tea" in the middle of the afternoon.

Rubber spatulas tend to be easier to use than a knife or metal spatula because the rubber ones are not as likely to cut into the cupcake.

Coconut Delight Cupcakes ▶

Chocolate-Strawberry Cupcakes

1 (18 ounce) box milk chocolate cake mix
⅓ cup canola oil
3 eggs
1 teaspoon almond extract
1 cup white chocolate chips

 Preheat oven to 350°.

 Place paper baking cups in 24 muffin cups. Combine cake mix, 1¼ cups water, oil, eggs and almond extract in bowl.

 Beat on low speed for 30 seconds; increase speed to medium and beat for 2 minutes. Stir in white chocolate chips and spoon into muffin cups.

Bake for 18 to 22 minutes or until toothpick inserted in center comes out clean. Cool for 10 minutes; then let cool completely for 30 minutes before frosting. Yields 24 cupcakes.

Decorations:

1 (16 ounce) container ready-to-serve strawberry frosting
1 (3 ounce) container chocolate jimmies or sprinkles

 Use a pastry bag fitted with an open star tip number 21. Squeeze bag evenly around cupcake from outside to inside. Top with sprinkles.

For a special touch, dip one whole strawberry with stem in melted chocolate about half-way to stem and place on top of cupcakes.

Cherry-Chocolate Cupcakes

1 (18 ounce) box devil's food chocolate cake mix
3 large eggs
⅓ cup oil
1 teaspoon almond extract
1 (6 ounce) bottle maraschino cherries,
　　　drained, chopped
1 cup white chocolate chips

 Preheat oven to 350°.

Place paper baking cups in 24 muffin cups.
Combine cake mix, eggs, oil, almond extract and
1¼ cups water in bowl and beat on low speed for
about 30 seconds. Increase speed to medium and
beat mixture for 2 minutes.

 Stir in cherries and white chocolate chips and mix
well, but gently.

 Pour into muffin cups and bake for 19 to 23 minutes
or until toothpick inserted in center comes out
clean. Cool on wire rack for 5 to 10 minutes; cool
completely before frosting. Yields 24 cupcakes.

Decorations:

1 (16 ounce) container ready-to-serve
　　　cherry frosting
1 (6 ounce) bottle maraschino cherries with stems

Spread cherry frosting over cupcakes using knife in
swirling motion and top with 1 cherry with stem.

Triple-Chocolate Cones

1 (18 ounce) box triple chocolate fudge cake mix
½ cup canola oil
2 eggs
1 cup chocolate chips
1 (24 count) box flat-bottomed ice cream cones

 Preheat oven to 350°.

 Combine cake mix, 1¼ cups water, oil and eggs in bowl. Beat on low speed for 30 seconds.

 Increase speed to medium and beat for 2 minutes. Stir in chocolate chips and spoon into cones within ½ inch of top. Place in muffin pan and place crumpled pieces of foil where needed to stabilize each cone.

 Bake for 19 to 23 minutes or until toothpick inserted in center comes out clean. Cool completely before frosting. Yields 24 cupcake cones.

Decorations:

1 (12 ounce) container ready-to-serve
        white frosting
1 (2 ounce) jar chocolate sprinkles

Use a pastry bag fitted with an open star tip or even a round tip. Squeeze bag evenly around cupcake from outside to inside. Top with chocolate sprinkles.

You can't change the past, but you can ruin the present by worrying over the future. Anonymous

Chocolate Cupcakes Topped with White Chocolate and Brickle Bits

1 (18 ounce) box devil's food cake mix
3 eggs
⅓ cup canola oil
1 cup chocolate chips

 Preheat oven to 350°.

 Place paper baking cups in 24 muffin cups. Combine cake mix, 1¼ cups water, eggs and oil in bowl and beat on low speed for 30 seconds.

 Increase speed to medium and beat for 2 minutes. Stir in chocolate chips and spoon batter into muffin cups.

 Bake for 21 to 25 minutes or until toothpick inserted in center comes out clean. Cool for 10 minutes before removing from pan. Cool completely before frosting. Yields 24 cupcakes.

Continued next page...

Ralph: Did you hear the joke about the broken egg?

Eddie: Yes, it cracked me up!

Continued from previous page...

Decorations:

**1 (16 ounce) container ready-to-serve creamy
           chocolate frosting
1 cup white chocolate chips
1 cup brickle bits**

 Microwave white chocolate chips in microwave-safe bowl on MEDIUM for about 2½ minutes and stir after 1 or 2 minutes. Stir until smooth and cool for 5 minutes. Stir in frosting until mixture blends well.

 Immediately frost cupcakes. Use a pastry bag fitted with an open star tip number 17 or 21. Squeeze bag evenly around cupcake from outside to inside.

 These cupcakes are extra pretty sprinkled with white chocolate shavings and brickle bits on top.

Always check cupcakes for doneness at the minimum baking time. Check for doneness by inserting a toothpick in the center. If it comes out clean or with just a few dry crumbs attached, your cupcake is done!

White Truffle-Chocolate Cupcakes

1 (18 ounce) box chocolate cake mix
3 large eggs
⅓ cup canola oil
1 teaspoon almond extract
⅓ cup flaked coconut
1 (12 ounce) package white chocolate chips

Preheat oven to 350°.

Place paper baking cups in 24 muffin cups. Combine cake mix, eggs, oil, almond extract and 1¼ cups water and beat on low speed for 30 seconds.

Increase speed to medium and beat for 2 minutes. Stir in coconut and white chocolate chips.

Pour into muffin cups and bake for 19 to 23 minutes. Cool in pan for about 5 minutes. Cool completely before frosting. Yields 24 cupcakes.

Decorations:

1 (16 ounce) container ready-to-serve fluffy white frosting
Food coloring, optional
1½ cups sweetened flaked coconut
1 (10 ounce) bar dark chocolate bar, shaved, optional
1 (10 ounce) bar white chocolate bar, shaved, optional

Use a pastry bag fitted with an open star tip number 17 or 21.

Continued next page...

Continued from previous page...

Squeeze bag evenly around cupcake from outside to inside. Sprinkle coconut on top and sides. Another idea is to sprinkle with chocolate shavings,

TIP: *To dye coconut, place a few drops of food color in small container and swirl it against the sides. Add coconut and mix well or cover container with lid and shake.*

TIP: *Hold chocolate bar on its side and use potato peeler to make chocolate curls and shavings.*

When asked what the meaning of life is, the old woman quickly answered, "Chocolate".

Just about any standard cake mix can be used to make cupcakes. The only real difference comes in the baking time. Because cupcakes are smaller, the cooking time is usually less than larger cakes.

White Truffle-Chocolate Cupcakes ▶

Cupcake Sundaes

1 (18 ounce) box milk chocolate cake mix
⅓ cup canola oil
3 eggs

 Preheat oven to 350°.

 Place paper baking cups in 24 muffin cups. Combine
cake mix, 1¼ cup water, oil and eggs in bowl.

 Beat on low speed for 30 seconds; increase speed
to medium and beat for 2 minutes. Spoon into
muffin cups.

 Bake for 19 to 22 minutes or until toothpick
inserted in center comes out clean. Cool for
5 minutes before removing from pan. Cool
completely before frosting. Yields 24 cupcakes.

Decorations:

½ cup vegetable oil
1 tablespoon egg white
2 tablespoons milk
3 cups powdered sugar, sifted
Chocolate syrup
1 (6 ounce) jar maraschino cherries with stems

 Lightly beat vegetable oil, egg white and milk in
large bowl. Add half powdered sugar and beat.
Add remaining powdered sugar and beat on high
for several minutes.

Use ice cream scoop to put frosting on cupcake.
Drizzle chocolate syrup over cupcake and top
with cherry.

Chocolate-Filled Cupcakes

1 (18 ounce) box devil's food cake mix
1⅓ cups buttermilk*
4 eggs, divided
⅓ cup canola oil
1 cup mini semi-sweet chocolate chips, divided
1 (8 ounce) package cream cheese, softened
½ cup sugar

 Preheat oven to 350°.

 Combine cake mix, buttermilk, 3 eggs and oil in large bowl. Beat on low speed to blend, then beat on medium for 2 minutes. Stir ½ cup chocolate chips into batter.

 In separate bowl, beat cream cheese, sugar and remaining egg until mixture is smooth. Melt remaining chocolate chips in saucepan and add to cream cheese mixture. Beat mixture until it blends well.

 Prepare 24 muffin cups by either spraying and flouring or using paper baking liners. Fill each muffin cup half full with batter.

 Drop 1 tablespoon chocolate-cream cheese mixture in center and spoon remaining batter evenly over filling. Bake for 25 minutes or until toothpick inserted in center comes out clean. Yields 24 cupcakes.

*TIP: To make buttermilk, mix 1 cup milk with 1 tablespoon lemon juice or vinegar and let milk stand for about 10 minutes.

Creme-Filled Chocolate Cupcakes

1 (18 ounce) box double chocolate cake mix
½ cup canola oil
1 egg

 Preheat oven to 350°.

Place paper baking cups in 24 muffin cups. Stir cake mix, 1 cup water, oil and egg in medium bowl just until they blend and divide batter among muffin cups.

Bake for 18 to 22 minutes. Cool in pan for 10 minutes, remove from pan and cool completely. Yields 24 cupcakes.

Decorations:

1 (16 ounce) container ready-to-serve
     vanilla frosting
1 cup marshmallow creme
Powdered sugar, optional
Fresh fruit, optional

 Combine vanilla frosting and marshmallow creme in bowl; mix well.

 Cut tops off cupcakes.

 Use a pastry bag fitted with an open star tip number 17 or 21. Squeeze bag evenly around bottom part of cupcake from outside to inside.

Continued next page...

Continued from previous page...

 Replace top of cupcake, sprinkle with powdered sugar and garnish with fresh fruit.

January 27: Chocolate Cake Day!

More statistical studies are finding that family meals play a significant role in childhood development. Children who eat with their families four or more nights per week are healthier, make better grades in school, score higher on aptitude tests and are less likely to have problems with drugs.

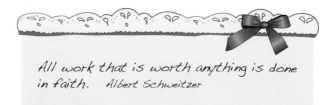

All work that is worth anything is done in faith. Albert Schweitzer

Chocolate-Peanut Butter Cupcakes

1¾ cups flour
1 tablespoon cocoa
2 teaspoons baking powder
¾ cup peanut butter
½ cup (1 stick) butter, softened
1½ cups sugar
2 eggs
¾ cup milk
1 teaspoon vanilla

 Preheat oven to 350°.

 Place paper baking cups in 20 muffin cups. Whisk flour, cocoa and baking powder in medium bowl.

 In separate bowl, beat peanut butter and butter until smooth. Add sugar gradually and beat thoroughly. Add eggs, one at a time, beating well after each addition, about 2 minutes.

Add flour mixture, alternating with milk, beginning and ending with flour mixture. Stir in vanilla. Divide batter equally among muffin cups.

Bake for 24 to 26 minutes or until toothpick inserted in center comes out clean. Remove from pan and cool completely on wire rack. Yields 20 cupcakes.

Continued next page...

December 15th is National Cupcake Day!

Continued from previous page...

Decorations:

1 (16 ounce) container ready-to-serve
        milk chocolate frosting
½ cup peanut butter
Mini chocolate candies or sprinkles
Miniature jelly beans or equivalent

   Combine milk chocolate frosting and peanut
        butter in bowl and mix well.

   Use a pastry bag fitted with an open star tip
        number 21 or 22. Leave some cupcake showing
        and squeeze bag evenly around cupcake from
        outside to inside. Decorate with sprinkles, jelly
        beans, etc.

*Hostess CupCakes were first made in
1919, but they were a small snack cake.
It wasn't until 1950 when they were
filled with a crème center that they
became the Hostess CupCakes of today.*

Bad decisions make good stories.

Chocolate-Peanut Butter Cupcakes ▶

Chocolate-Peanut Butter Yummies

1 (21 ounce) package double fudge brownie mix
2 eggs
3 (9 ounce) packages miniature peanut
     butter cups

 Preheat oven to 350°.

 Prepare brownie mix according to package
     directions using 2 eggs. Spoon into 8 miniature
     foil cupcake liners and fill three-fourths full.

Place peanut butter cup in center of each and
push into batter. Bake for 20 to 25 minutes or
until toothpick inserted in center comes out clean.
Yields 8 cupcakes.

Decorations:

1 (16 ounce) container ready-to-serve
     buttercream frosting
½ cup peanut butter
1 (2 ounce) jar chocolate sprinkles
½ cup peanuts
Miniature peanut butter cups

 Place buttercream frosting in small bowl, stir
     in peanut butter and mix well. Spread frosting
     generously over cupcakes.

 Turn cupcake on its side and roll edge in chocolate
     sprinkles. Place peanuts in frosting and top with
     peanut butter cup halves.

Chocolate Fudge Cupcakes

1 (18 ounce) box butter-fudge cake mix
3 large eggs
⅓ cup canola oil
1 (6 ounce) package butter-brickle chips

 Preheat oven to 350°.

 Place paper baking cups in 24 muffin cups.
Combine cake mix, eggs, oil and 1¼ cups water in
bowl and beat on low speed for about 30 seconds.

 Increase speed to medium and beat for 2 minutes.
Stir in butter-brickle chips. Fill muffin cups
two-thirds full. Bake for 19 to 23 minutes.

 Cool on wire rack before removing from pan. Cool
completely before frosting. Yields 24 cupcakes.

Decorations:

1 (16 ounce) container ready-to-serve
            buttercream frosting
½ cup peanut butter
24 chocolate covered peanuts
Ground cinnamon or nutmeg

 Place buttercream frosting in small bowl, stir in
peanut butter and mix well.

 Use a pastry bag fitted with a round tip number
8 or 10. Squeeze bag evenly around cupcake
from outside to inside. Sprinkle with cinnamon
or nutmeg and top with chocolate-covered peanut.

Devil's Chocolate Cupcakes

1 (18 ounce) box devil's food cake mix
⅓ cup canola oil
3 large eggs
1 cup cold milk
1 (3.4 ounce) box instant vanilla pudding mix
½ cup peanut butter

 Preheat oven to 350°.

 Place paper baking cups in 24 muffin cups. Combine cake mix, oil, eggs and 1 cup water and beat for 2½ minutes.

 In separate bowl, combine cold milk and pudding mix. Whisk for 2 minutes or until creamy and mixture blends well. Stir in peanut butter and mix well. Stir mixture into cake mix-eggs mixture.

 Spoon into muffin cups and bake for 19 to 22 minutes or until toothpick inserted in center comes out clean. Cool for 10 minutes in pan; cool completely before frosting. Yields 24 cupcakes.

Decorations:

1 (16 ounce) container milk chocolate frosting
Chopped nuts, butter-brickle bits or toffee bits

 Spread chocolate frosting over cupcakes using a pastry bag fitted with a large star tip. Sprinkle with nuts, butter-brickle bits or toffee bits.

For a different look, use 1 (16 ounce) container vanilla funfetti frosting. That will give these cupcakes a "fun" look!

Rich Brownie Cupcakes

1 cup (2 sticks) unsalted butter
½ cup cocoa
½ cup sugar
1 cup packed brown sugar
3 eggs
1 teaspoon vanilla
1 cup flour
1 cup chopped pecans

 Preheat oven to 350°.

 Place paper baking cups in 16 muffin cups. Melt butter in large saucepan, stir in cocoa and stir until smooth. Add sugar and brown sugar, mix well and remove from heat.

 Add eggs and vanilla and beat well. Stir in flour and pecans until they blend well. Fill prepared muffin cups about three-fourths full.

Bake for 21 to 25 minutes or until toothpick inserted in center comes out clean. Cool completely on wire rack. Yields 16 cupcakes.

Decorations:

1 (12 ounce) container ready-to-serve
      chocolate frosting
1 (2 ounce) bottle candy confetti, optional

Use a pastry bag fitted with a closed star tip number 28 or 30. Squeeze bag evenly around cupcake from outside to inside. Sprinkle frosting with candy confetti.

Double Rich Chocolate Cupcakes

½ cup cocoa
1⅔ cups flour
1½ cups sugar
½ teaspoon baking soda
½ cup shortening
2 eggs
1 (6 ounce) package chocolate chips

 Preheat oven to 350°.

 Place paper baking cups in 24 muffin cups. Mix cocoa and 1 cup hot water in bowl with spoon until mixture is smooth. Let mixture cool for about 10 minutes.

 Add flour, sugar, baking soda, shortening and eggs and beat on low speed for 2 minutes. Increase speed and beat for additional 2 minutes. Stir in chocolate chips and mix well. Fill muffin cups half full.

 Bake for 18 to 20 minutes or until toothpick inserted in center comes out clean. Cool completely before frosting. Yields 24 cupcakes.

Decorations:

1 (16 ounce) container ready-to-serve
        dark chocolate frosting
Pink sprinkles or jimmies

 Use a pastry bag fitted with a closed star tip number 28 or 30.

Continued next page...

Continued from previous page...

 Squeeze bag evenly around cupcake from outside to inside. Top with pink sprinkles.

TIP: Grab a chocolate bar and slice chocolate curls with a potato peeler to put on top of the dark chocolate frosting. You will have Triple Chocolate Chocolate Chocolate Cupcakes!

Let butter come to room temperature before using it. The texture of the product will be better if butter is soft than if you mix cold butter or melted butter with ingredients.

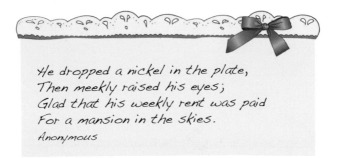

He dropped a nickel in the plate,
Then meekly raised his eyes;
Glad that his weekly rent was paid
For a mansion in the skies.
Anonymous

Double Divine Cupcakes

2 cups flour
⅔ cup cocoa
1¼ teaspoons baking soda
¾ cup (1½ sticks) unsalted butter, softened
2 cups sugar
2 large eggs, beaten
1 teaspoon vanilla
½ cup buttermilk*
½ cup chopped pecans or walnuts

 Preheat oven to 350°.

 Place paper baking cups in 16 muffin cups.
Combine flour, cocoa, baking soda and
¼ teaspoon salt in bowl.

 In separate bowl, beat butter and sugar until
fluffy; stir in eggs and vanilla. Fold in flour
mixture alternately with buttermilk and end with
flour mixture. Stir in chopped pecans or walnuts.

 Spoon into muffin cups and bake for 20 to
22 minutes or until toothpick inserted in center
comes out clean. Allow to cool for 10 minutes
in pan. Cool completely before frosting. Yields
16 cupcakes.

Decorations:

1 (12 ounce) container ready-to-serve milk
            chocolate frosting
Ground nuts

Use a pastry bag fitted with a closed star tip
number 17 or 21.

Continued next page...

Continued from previous page...

 Squeeze bag evenly around cupcake from outside to inside. Sprinkle nuts on top.

*TIP: To make buttermilk, mix 1 cup milk with 1 tablespoon lemon juice or vinegar and let milk stand for about 10 minutes.

The first users of cacao were probably the Olmecs, the oldest known civilization in the Americas, which existed from 1500 BC to about 400 BC.

When we gather at the dinner table, we form bonds that translate into who we are and where we come from. For one brief moment when we sit down to enjoy a meal, carry on conversations and listen to each other, we become a true family.

Double Divine Cupcakes ▶

Chocolate-Coconut Cupcakes

2 cups flour
¾ cup sugar
3 tablespoons cocoa
1 tablespoon baking powder
1 cup milk
1 egg
⅓ cup canola oil
1½ cups flaked coconut, divided
¼ cup sweetened condensed milk
¼ teaspoon almond extract

Preheat oven to 350°.

Place paper baking cups in 14 muffin cups.
Combine flour, sugar, cocoa, baking powder and
½ teaspoon salt in large bowl. In separate bowl,
combine milk, egg and oil and mix well.

Pour milk-egg mixture into dry ingredients and
stir just until moist. Spoon 2 tablespoonfuls into
muffin cups.

Combine 1 cup coconut, sweetened condensed
milk and almond extract in bowl and place
2 teaspoonfuls in center of batter of each cupcake.
(Do not spread.) Top with remaining batter and
sprinkle with remaining coconut.

Bake for 20 to 23 minutes or until toothpick
inserted in cupcake comes out clean. Cool in
pan for about 5 minutes. Place cupcakes on
wire rack to cool completely before frosting.
Yields 14 cupcakes.

Continued next page...

Continued from previous page...

Decorations:

1 (12 ounce) container ready-to-serve
        chocolate frosting
1 (14 ounce) package sweetened flaked coconut

Spread frosting over each cupcake. Sprinkle
coconut on top of frosting.

Cupcakes were called "fairy cakes"
in England because they were made in
teacups. Small, delicate cakes baked
in teacups seemed exactly like what
fairies would serve at parties.

Hostess CupCakes are the best-selling
cupcakes in the U.S. Americans eat
more than 500 million Hostess CupCakes
every year.

Cocoa-Macaroon Cupcakes

3 egg whites, divided
1 egg
⅓ cup applesauce
1 teaspoon vanilla
1¼ cups flour
1¼ cups sugar, divided
⅓ cup cocoa
½ teaspoon baking soda
¾ cup buttermilk*
1 cup ricotta cheese
1 (14 ounce) package sweetened flaked
    coconut, divided

 Preheat oven to 350°.

 Place paper baking cups in 18 muffin cups. Combine 2 egg whites, 1 whole egg, applesauce and vanilla in bowl.

 In separate bowl, combine flour, 1 cup sugar, cocoa and baking soda and gradually add to egg white mixture alternately with buttermilk.

 Place half batter into muffin cups. Beat ricotta cheese, remaining sugar and remaining egg white in bowl until mixture is smooth. Stir in half coconut.

Spoon 1 tablespoon ricotta mixture in center of batter in each muffin cup; fill each muffin cup with remaining batter. Bake for 26 to 30 minutes or until toothpick inserted in center comes out clean.

Continued next page...

Continued from previous page...

 Cool for 5 minutes before removing from pan.
Cool completely before frosting cupcakes.
These cupcakes need to be refrigerated.
Yields 18 cupcakes.

Decorations:

**1 (14 ounce) container ready-to-serve
        caramel frosting
Remaining coconut from cupcake recipe**

 Spread thick layer of frosting over each cupcake.
Sprinkle coconut on top.

**TIP: To make buttermilk, mix 1 cup milk with
         1 tablespoon lemon juice or vinegar and let
         milk stand for about 10 minutes.*

*Using an ice cream scoop that holds
about ¼ to ⅓ cup of cupcake batter
makes filling cupcake pans much
faster. Pans should be filled about
three-quarters full.*

Nestlé introduced chocolate chips in 1939.

Cocoa-Macaroon Cupcakes ▶

Nutty Red Velvet Cupcakes

1 (18 ounce) box red velvet cake mix
3 eggs
⅓ cup canola oil
1 (6 ounce) package white chocolate chips
½ cup chopped walnuts

 Preheat oven to 350°.

 Place paper baking cups in 24 muffin cups. Blend cake mix, 1¼ cups water, eggs and oil in bowl on low speed for 30 seconds.

 Beat on medium speed for 2 minutes. Stir in white chocolate chips and walnuts and pour into muffin cups.

Bake for 19 to 23 minutes or until toothpick inserted in center in center comes out clean. Let stand on wire rack for 30 minutes. Remove each cupcake from pan and cool completely before frosting. Yields 24 cupcakes.

Decorations:

1 (16 ounce) container ready-to-serve
    whipped frosting

 Use a pastry bag fitted with a closed star tip number 28 or 30 or just use a knife in a swirling motion.

Easy Birthday Cupcakes

1 (18 ounce) box milk chocolate cake mix
⅓ cup canola oil
3 eggs
¼ cup chopped pecans

 Preheat oven to 350°.

 Place paper baking cups in 24 muffin cups.
Combine cake mix, 1¼ cups water, oil and eggs
in large bowl.

 Beat on low speed for 30 seconds. Increase
speed to medium and beat for 2 minutes. Stir in
chopped pecans and spoon into muffin cups.

 Bake for 18 to 22 minutes or until toothpick placed
in center comes out clean. Cool in pan for 5 to
10 minutes. Cool completely before frosting.
Yields 24 cupcakes.

Decorations:

1 (14 ounce) container ready-to-serve
                buttercream frosting
Candy birthday toppers or heart toppers, optional

Use a pastry bag fitted with a round tip number
7 or 10. Squeeze bag evenly around cupcake from
outside to inside. Place candy topper in center.

*Birthdays are nature's way of telling us
to eat more cake.*

Happy Hearts Cupcakes

1 (18 ounce) box milk chocolate cake mix
⅓ cup canola oil
3 eggs

 Preheat oven to 350°.

 Place paper baking cups in 24 muffin cups. Combine cake mix, 1¼ cups water, oil and eggs in bowl. Beat on low speed for 30 seconds. Increase speed and beat for 2 minutes.

 Spoon into muffin cups and bake for 19 to 22 minutes or until toothpick inserted into center comes out clean.

Cool for 5 minutes before removing from pan. Cool completely before frosting. Yields 24 cupcakes.

Decorations:

½ cup vegetable oil
1 tablespoon egg white
2 tablespoons milk
3 cups powdered sugar
Red food coloring
Heart toppers, optional
Nonpareils, optional

Lightly beat vegetable oil, egg white and milk in large bowl. Add half powdered sugar and beat for a few seconds. Add remaining powdered sugar and beat on high for several minutes. (Be careful not to beat the fluff out of the frosting.)

Continued next page...

Continued from previous page...

 Place big dollop of frosting on top of cupcake. Add one drop of red food coloring to remaining frosting and mix.

 Place frosting in pastry bag fitted with an open star tip number 22 or 32. Squeeze bag to form star at very top. Decorating with heart toppers and nonpareils is optional.

Frosting Recipes are available on 144-156.

Batter for an 8-inch cake pan makes about 20 cupcakes. Fill cupcake molds about ⅔ to ¾ full and bake at 350° for about 20 minutes or until toothpick inserted in center comes out clean.

The origin and creator of cupcakes cannot be pinpointed in culinary history, but it can be assumed that the name "cupcake" derived from its measurements.

The basic cupcake recipe started out with 1 cup butter, 1 cup sugar and 1 cup flour. This was similar to the traditional pound cake named for its measurements of 1 pound butter, 1 pound sugar, 1 pound flour and 1 pound eggs.

Another theory is that cupcakes were named for how they were baked. Instead of a large cake pan, cups and small earthenware vessels were used to make individual cakes.

The individual cake idea seems to be an American idea because cupcakes, as opposed to muffins, never really caught on in countries east of the Atlantic. Small cakes were not the sweet dessert treats they were in America. The term "sweet" took on a new dimension as more sugar, molasses and honey were added to baked goods in America.

Easter-Ready Cupcakes

1 (18 ounce) box yellow cake mix
⅓ cup canola oil
3 eggs

 Preheat oven to 350°.

 Place fancy paper baking cups in 24 muffin cups.
Combine cake mix, 1¼ cups water, oil and eggs in
bowl. Beat on low speed for 30 seconds.

 Increase speed to medium and beat for 2 minutes.
Spoon batter into muffin cups. Bake for 19 to
22 minutes or until toothpick inserted in center
comes out clean. Cool in pan for 5 minutes. Cool
completely before frosting. Yields 24 cupcakes.

Decorations:

1 (16 ounce) container ready-to-serve classic
white frosting
Green food coloring
72 candy eggs

Place frosting in bowl. Add a drop or two of
green food coloring and mix to get right color.
Squeeze frosting in a pattern of grass on each
cupcake using a pastry bag fitted with multi-
opening tip (such as Wilton tip #233). Place
3 candy eggs in middle of grass. (Jelly beans
would also work great.)

TIP: To make "grass" you need a thick frosting. Do a trial
run on wax paper before you get started. If frosting
isn't thick enough, add powdered sugar until the
texture is right.

Fourth of July Celebration

1 (18 ounce) box yellow cake mix
⅓ cup canola oil
3 eggs
1 cup M&M's® chocolate mini baking bits

 Preheat oven to 350°.

Place paper baking cups in 24 muffin cups.
Combine cake mix, 1¼ cups water, oil and eggs
in bowl and beat on low speed for 30 seconds.

Increase speed to medium and beat for 2 minutes.
Fold in M&M's® and spoon into muffin cups.

Bake for 18 to 20 minutes or until toothpick
inserted in center comes out clean. Cool for
5 to 10 minutes in pan. Cool completely before
frosting. Yields 24 cupcakes.

Decorations:

1 (16 ounce) container ready-to-serve
    white frosting
1 (4 ounce) bottle blue and red star-shaped
    sprinkles
2 (12 count) packages small sparklers

 Spread frosting over cupcakes with a pastry
bag fitted with a closed star tip number 28 or
30. Sprinkle generously with red and blue stars.
Finish with a small sparkler.

Spice Up the Holidays

1 (18 ounce) box spice cake mix
1 (15 ounce) can pumpkin
3 large eggs
⅓ cup canola oil
½ teaspoon ground cinnamon
⅔ cup chopped pecans

 Preheat oven to 350°.

 Place paper baking cups in 24 muffin cups. Combine cake mix, pumpkin, eggs, oil, cinnamon and ⅓ cup water in bowl and beat on low speed for 30 seconds.

 Increase speed to medium and beat for 2 minutes. Stir in chopped pecans and fill muffin cups three-fourth full with batter.

 Bake for 19 to 23 minutes or until toothpick inserted in center comes out clean. Cool for 10 minutes before removing from pan. Cool completely before frosting. Yields 24 cupcakes.

Decorations:

1 (16 ounce) container ready-to-serve
          buttercream frosting
24 sugar or fondant gingerbread men, optional

 Use a pastry bag fitted with an open star number 17 or 21. Squeeze bag evenly around cupcake from outside to inside.

 Place 1 gingerbread man topper in center.

Christmas Cheer Cupcakes

1 (18 ounce) box white cake mix
⅓ cup canola oil
4 egg whites
½ cup Craisins®

 Preheat oven to 350°.

Place paper baking cups in 24 muffin cups. Combine cake mix, 1¼ cups water, oil and egg whites in bowl and beat on low speed for 30 seconds.

 Increase speed to medium and beat for 2 to 2½ minutes. Stir in Craisins® and spoon into muffin cups. (If you want the frosting to be even with the cupcake liner, only fill halfway with batter.)

 Bake for 18 to 22 minutes or until toothpick inserted in center comes out clean. Cool in pan for about 5 minutes. Remove from pan and cool completely before frosting. Yields 24 cupcakes.

Decorations:

1 (16 ounce) container ready-to-serve fluffy white frosting or white fondant
24 candy or fondant Christmas toppers

 Spread white frosting smoothly over tops of cupcakes and add your favorite topper.

 There are lots of "candy" figures that you can buy that will represent lots of themes. Search for your theme in hobby, craft or baking supply stores and you will have a figure for every theme of the year.

Traditional Buttercream Frosting

½ cup shortening
½ cup unsalted butter
1 teaspoon vanilla
2 tablespoons milk
4 cups powdered sugar, sifted

Mix all ingredients until creamy. For pure white frosting, use 1 cup shortening and no butter. Add ½ teaspoon butter flavoring and 3 tablespoons corn syrup, water or milk. Frosting for 18 cupcakes.

Frosting is a mixture of sugar, butter, and water or milk and has a thick consistency so that it will hold its shape.

Icing is thinner than frosting and dries with a fairly smooth surface. It works well for decorating and is better for decorating tips with small holes.

Glaze is a very thin powdered sugar-water or milk mixture that is drizzled over cupcakes.

In Easy Cupcakes we use the term frosting to include icing.

Decorator Frosting

2 cups powdered sugar, sifted
¼ cup plus 2 tablespoons solid vegetable
**   shortening, room temperature**
2 tablespoons milk
½ teaspoon almond extract
Food coloring

 Beat powdered sugar, shortening, milk, almond extract and pinch of salt in bowl on low speed until smooth and creamy.

 Start with 1 small drop of your favorite food coloring. Add more if needed for deeper color. Frosting for 24 cupcakes.

You know you're getting old when you get that one candle on the cake. It's like, "See if you can blow this out."
Jerry Seinfeld

Place icing on top of cupcakes and spread from the top down to the edge to keep crumbs out of the icing.

Brown Sugar Icing

½ cup (1 stick) unsalted butter
1 cup packed brown sugar
¼ cup milk
1¾ - 2 cups powdered sugar
½ teaspoon vanilla

 Melt butter in heavy saucepan, add brown sugar and milk and cook for about 3 minutes, stirring constantly. Cool for 10 minutes.

 Add 1¾ cups powdered sugar and vanilla; beat until creamy. If needed, add more powdered sugar to make spreadable consistency. Frosting for 24 cupcakes.

Champion Cream Frosting

¾ cup (1½ sticks) unsalted butter, softened
⅓ cup sour cream
4 - 4½ cups powdered sugar, sifted
1 teaspoon vanilla

 Beat butter, sour cream and pinch of salt in bowl until creamy. Gradually add 4 cups powdered sugar and beat until light and fluffy.

 Add more powdered sugar if needed for spreading consistency. Stir in vanilla and mix well. Refrigerate. Frosting for 24 cupcakes.

Deluxe Cream Cheese Frosting

1 (8 ounce) package cream cheese, softened
½ cup (1 stick) unsalted butter, softened
1 (16 ounce) box powdered sugar
¾ teaspoon almond extract
1½ cups chopped pecans

 Beat cream cheese and butter in bowl on medium speed until smooth and creamy. Reduce speed to low, gradually add powdered sugar and beat until light and fluffy.

 Stir in almond extract and pecans. Refrigerate. Frosting for 24 cupcakes.

Rich Vanilla Frosting

1¼ cups (2½ sticks) unsalted butter, softened
2 tablespoons whipping cream
1 teaspoon vanilla
2½ - 2¾ cups powdered sugar

 Beat butter in bowl on medium-high speed for about 1 minute or until smooth. Stir in cream, vanilla and a pinch of salt and mix well.

 Reduce speed to medium-low and gradually add powdered sugar; beat until mixture is light and fluffy. Refrigerate. Frosting for 24 cupcakes.

Velvet Whipped Cream Frosting

1½ cups whipping cream
3 tablespoons cocoa
5 tablespoons powdered sugar
½ teaspoon vanilla

 Beat cream, cocoa, powdered sugar and vanilla in bowl on medium-high speed until soft peaks form. Refrigerate. Frosting for 14 to 15 cupcakes.

Icing methods for cupcakes can be quick and simple or you can try your hand at cupcake decorating, which requires extra time and attention and can be lots of fun. To make cupcake decorating easier, see the tips throughout this cookbook.

I totally take back all those times I didn't want to take a nap when I was younger.

Kahlua-Chocolate Frosting

¼ cup (½ stick) unsalted butter, softened
1 (8 ounce) package cream cheese, softened
1 (16 ounce) box powdered sugar, sifted, divided
2 (1 ounce) squares unsweetened chocolate,
       melted, cooled
¼ cup Kahlua® liqueur*

 Beat butter and cream cheese in bowl until creamy. Add 1 cup powdered sugar and melted chocolate and beat until creamy.

 Gradually add remaining powdered sugar and Kahlua®. Beat on low speed until spreading consistency. Refrigerate. Frosting for 24 cupcakes.

*TIP: If you don't want to use Kahlua®, just use ¼ cup strong, brewed coffee instead.

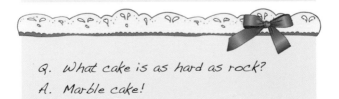

It is best to add 1 teaspoon butter to chocolate when melting it because it will give it a better consistency.

Q. What cake is as hard as rock?
A. Marble cake!

Dark Chocolate Frosting

1¼ cups (2½ sticks) unsalted butter, softened
8 (1 ounce) squares semi-sweet chocolate,
    melted
1 teaspoon vanilla
1 (16 ounce) box powdered sugar
2 tablespoons cocoa

 Beat butter in bowl on medium speed until
smooth. Stir in melted chocolate, vanilla and
pinch of salt.

In separate bowl, combine powdered sugar and
cocoa. Gradually add sugar-cocoa mixture to
butter mixture and beat until light and fluffy.
Frosting for 24 cupcakes.

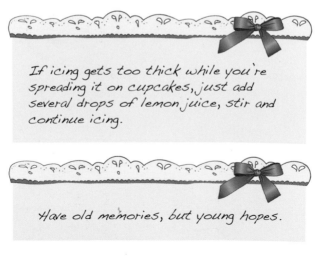

*If icing gets too thick while you're
spreading it on cupcakes, just add
several drops of lemon juice, stir and
continue icing.*

Have old memories, but young hopes.

Creamy Mocha Icing

1 tablespoon instant coffee granules
½ cup (1 stick) unsalted butter, softened
3 tablespoons cocoa
4¼ cups powdered sugar, sifted, divided
1 teaspoon vanilla

 Dissolve coffee granules in ¼ cup hot water and let cool for about 10 minutes. Beat butter and cocoa in bowl on medium speed until creamy.

 Gradually add 4 cups powdered sugar alternately with coffee mixture, beginning and ending with powdered sugar.

 Add more powdered sugar if needed for spreading consistency. Stir in vanilla and mix well. Frosting for 24 cupcakes.

Add a little baking soda to powdered sugar when making icing so the icing will not dry out as quickly.

December 16th is National Chocolate-Covered Anything Day!

Sweet Coffee-Cocoa Icing

½ cup (1 stick) unsalted butter
¾ cup cocoa
¼ cup cold brewed coffee
1 teaspoon vanilla
1 (16 ounce) box powdered sugar

 Beat butter in bowl on medium speed until very light. Stir in cocoa, coffee, vanilla, a pinch of salt and powdered sugar; blend thoroughly. Frosting for 24 cupcakes.

TIP: *If you want a stronger coffee flavor, stir about 1 or 2 tablespoons instant coffee granules into the brewed coffee.*

Peanut Butter Icing

2 cups powdered sugar
3 tablespoons peanut butter
1 teaspoon cinnamon
1 teaspoon nutmeg
4 - 6 tablespoons milk

 Combine all ingredients except milk. Add milk slowly until right consistency to spread. Frosting for 18 cupcakes.

Nutty Buttercream Icing

1 (3 ounce) package cream cheese, softened
6 tablespoons (¾ stick) unsalted butter, softened
1 tablespoon milk
1 teaspoon vanilla
2 cups powdered sugar
½ cup chopped pecans

 Beat cream cheese and butter in bowl. Stir in milk, vanilla, powdered sugar and pecans. Frosting for 18 cupcakes.

Easy frosting: Just dip the top of the cupcake in a bowl of frosting and swirl until covered.

Topping a cupcake with fondant creates a firm, level platform for decorating.

Caramel Icing

2 cups packed brown sugar
1 cup sugar
1 cup sour cream or milk
1 tablespoon unsalted butter
1 teaspoon vanilla
Cream

 Combine sugar, brown sugar and sour cream in large saucepan and cook slowly until sugars dissolve. Cook until a little of the mixture dropped in cold water forms soft ball (234° on candy thermometer).

 Remove from heat, add butter and vanilla, and cool to 145° or until outside of saucepan feels warm to the touch.

Beat until quite stiff, then add enough cream while beating to make spreading consistency. Frosting for 18 cupcakes.

Sprinkle powdered sugar over top of cupcake before icing to keep icing in place.

Dutch Apple-Nut Crumble Topping

½ cup packed brown sugar
2 tablespoons unsalted butter, softened
2 tablespoons flour
Dash ground nutmeg
Dash ground cinnamon
½ - ¾ cup chopped nuts

 Cream brown sugar and butter, add remaining ingredients and mix well. Crumble over top of cupcakes while still hot. Tops 18 cupcakes.

Creamy Lemon Filling

1 (14 ounce) can sweetened condensed milk
2 teaspoons grated lemon peel
Scant ⅓ cup lemon juice
¼ teaspoon vanilla
2 - 4 drops yellow food coloring
1½ cups frozen whipped topping, thawed

Combine sweetened condensed milk, lemon peel, lemon juice, vanilla and 2 drops food coloring. Stir well with wire whisk.

Slowly fold in whipped topping and mix until it blends well. Add more food coloring if desired. Refrigerate. Yields 3 cups.

Lemon Meringue

2 egg whites
¼ cup sugar
1 teaspoon lemon juice

Beat egg whites frothy. Continue beating while adding sugar gradually until egg white mixture holds its shape in peaks. Fold in lemon juice.

Spread on baked cupcakes. Use spoon to make peaks and bake just long enough to brown peaks. Tops 18 cupcakes.

STRESSED spelled backwards is DESSERTS.

We hope everyone recognizes the importance of sharing time and meals together. If you do, our families will be stronger, our nation will be stronger and our own little part of the world will feel a little safer and a little more loving. *The Publisher*

How to Use a Pastry Bag or a Plastic Bag to Decorate

A pastry bag is a cone-shaped bag with a small hole for a decorating tip on one end and a larger hole on the other end to fill bag with frosting.

Before adding the frosting, insert tip into bag and through small hole. Screw coupler ring of tip on outside of bag around tip. Make sure it is airtight with no way for frosting to leak out.

Fill bag half-way with frosting and twist at the top to seal. Slowly squeeze frosting through tip and decorate.

Make Your Own Pastry Bag

M ake your own pastry bag with a medium-size plastic bag. Cut small hole in one of the bottom corners. Repeat steps for pastry bag.

You don't have to have special tips unless you want pretty swirls and designs.

November 10th is National Vanilla Cupcake Day!

Decorating Ideas

There are literally thousands of ideas that make decorating fun, exciting and very creative. You can probably think of more things than we can come up with, but just to get you started, here are some great ideas.

Edible Decorations:

- Frostings and icings
- Food colors: liquids, oils, pastes, gels and powders
- Sprinkles
- Nonpareils (shiny little candy balls)
- Meringues: Mountain peaks at ski resort, Santa's beard, snow
- Candies: Facial features, borders for roads, ski slopes or paths, mountains, Indian tepees, rainbows
- Chocolate chips (all sizes).
- Chocolate shavings (dark chocolate and white chocolate): White caps on water, clouds
- Cookies and cookie crumbs
- Sugars: brown, granulated, powdered
- Chow mein noodles
- Fruits and veggies
- Nuts
- Flaked coconut
- Spices: cinnamon
- Fresh herbs-mint and parsley leaves
- Cinnamon sticks
- Honey

- Sauces: caramel, fudge, chocolate
- Pie fillings
- Marshmallows
- Edible glitter, sugars and sprinkles
- Fillings
- Dragees and edible pearls
- Ice cream cones

Non-Edible Decorations:

- Cupcake paper liners, foils, wraps
- Stencils
- Candy molds
- Cupcake and muffin pans
- Cookie cutters
- Ribbons
- Candles
- Small toys
- Cake toppers
- Beads
- Ice cream sticks
- Toothpicks
- Flowers
- Stationery and monograms
- Decorative trays, towers, stands and plates (or create your own with wrapping paper/ stationery and cardboard boxes)

As a general guideline, if you are having trouble creating the decorations you want and you feel your icing is too thin, add a little more powdered sugar; if you feel your icing is too thick, add a little more liquid.

Inspiration Gallery

Raffa Dowling of Cupcake Kingdom (www.cupcakekingdom.com) decorates beautiful cupcakes to inspire original ideas. Her Inspiration Gallery will jog your brain to come up with some easy, creative ideas of your own. The most important ingredient for cupcakes is fun!

A Cheeseburger Cupcake

A basic cupcake is cut in half. Green lettuce is made with green icing with a number 5 or 8 round tip.

The meat patty is made with a center cut from a chocolate cupcake. The cheese is made from yellow fondant. The tomato is fondant and the sesame seeds are chocolate sprinkles.

Blue Bow

White icing and colored crystallized sugar or sprinkles cover the cupcake.

Continued next page...

Continued from previous page...

The blue bow was made with straight lines cut from blue fondant which holds its shape well. All the parts were made from straight lines.

Honey Beehive

Frosting is dyed yellow and a number 11 or 12 round tip coupled to a pastry bag makes the rings of the hive. Stop squeezing when you reach the top and pull the pastry bag straight up.

The beehive is outlined in brown edible gel. The door, bees and wings are made with fondant. Thin black writing edible gel makes bees' faces.

Continued next page...

Continued from previous page...

Souvenir Basketball

Frosting is dyed orange and a thin layer is spread over shortbread or vanilla wafer cookies. Brown icing is piped on to create the basketball seams.

A buttercream frosting is swirled around the cupcake with a number 28 or 30 decorating tip and the basketball cookie is put in the icing at the top.

Beach Scene

The small umbrella is carried by craft, hobby and baking supply stores. The crab was made with fondant and its face was created with thin black writing gel.

The beach of buttercream frosting is first spread over the top of the cupcake with a knife. To make the sand, sprinkle graham cracker crumbs over the top. Insert umbrella and crab.

Shirt & Tie

Frost cupcake with number 28 or 30 closed star decorating tip.

Make a tie out of blue fondant. Add tie stripes and collar buttons made out of red fondant. The collar is made from white fondant.

Spaghetti and Meatballs

Let your kids laugh when they eat their spaghetti and meatballs.

A number 5 round tip will take care of the

spaghetti; the red sauce is just frosting dyed red. The meatballs can be made from fondant, stiff frosting or milk chocolate.

Continued next page...

Continued from previous page...

Sushi

Sushi anyone? The wasabi and ginger are made with green and pink frosting. The sushi "rice" was made with number 5 or 7 round tip.

The seaweed band and the shrimp are made from fondant. The bamboo "mat" is white frosting colored light brown with darker brown lines added.

Christmas Wreath

The Christmas wreath uses frosting (green food coloring) with an open star number 22 tip or a closed star number 33 decorating tip.

The red berries are made with a number 5 round tip. The bow is made from strips of red fondant.

Graduation

The frosting is a bed of red frosting using one of the smaller closed star tips or open star tips.

The white diploma is white fondant. It could also be made with thick frosting.

The graduation cap, tassel and bow are made with fondant. You can also buy an edible cap from a craft or hobby store.

Create colorful cupcakes by separating vanilla frosting into several bowls. Add a few drops of food coloring and you'll have plenty of different colors.

Maybe the little things, like having a meal at the table, are more important than we realize. Maybe these little things are really big things we never forget...big things like memories and family traditions that last a lifetime.

Selecting

Frosting	Description	Consistency
Buttercream	One of the most popular frostings; sweet with buttery flavor; excellent for decorating	Thin-to-stiff consistency; sugar stiffens frosting; corn syrup makes it thinner
Snow-White Buttercream	Similar to buttercream, but white color instead of egg-shell color; almond flavoring; excellent for wedding cupcakes	Thin-to-stiff consistency; sugar stiffens frosting; corn syrup makes it thinner
Ready-to-Use Decorator White	Sweet, vanilla flavor; pure white color	Thin-to-medium consistency; ready to spread
Ready-to-Use Decorator Chocolate	Sweet chocolate flavor; easy to use; great flavor	Stiff consistency; good for decorations that must hold shape such as roses
Royal	Very sweet; dries hard	Thin-to-stiff consistency; may be thinned with water
Ready-to-Use Rolled Fondant	Perfectly smooth appearance; used for wedding cakes; easy to use	Thick consistency similar to dough; cupcakes should be covered with glaze or thin icing to seal in moisture and to keep crumbs out of frosting

Frostings

Purpose	Characteristics
Smooth frostings; also good for borders, writing and all decorations	Can dye all colors; colors can deepen after setting; leftover frosting can be refrigerated for up to 10 days; decorations stay soft
Excellent for frostings with swirls; very good for all decorations and will stay soft	White base makes colors truer; colors will intensify after setting; leftover frosting can be refrigerated for up to 10 days
Convenience and time-saver; excellent flavor	White base makes colors truer; colors will intensify after setting; leftover frosting can be refrigerated for up to 10 days
Convenience and time-saver; excellent flavor; can be thinned with milk or water	Best to use for black or brown frostings; good coloring to chocolate for best flavor; leftover frosting can be refrigerated for up to 10 days;
Gets hard with time; excellent for detail; good for all decorations	Produces deeper colors than buttercream; decorations will last for several months; best to cover with damp cloth to prevent crusting
Best for perfect frostings, decorations; will hold its shape, but stay soft	White can be dyed all colors from pastel to deep colors; available in colors ready-to-use; leftover frosting may be stored for up to 2 months

Pan Sizes and Batter Amounts

Pan Size	Batter Amount	Estimated Baking Time @ 350°
Standard Muffin Pan	¼ to ⅓ cup per cupcake	18 to 20 minutes
Mini-Muffin Pan	1 heaping tablespoon	8 to 10 minutes
Jumbo Muffin Pan	½ to ⅔ cup	20 to 22 minutes
King-size Muffin Pan	⅞ cup	24 to 26 minutes

The best way to fill cupcake liners with batter is with an ice cream scoop or a melon baller for bite-size cupcakes.

Dark pans may cause cupcakes to cook a little faster or look a little darker.

To keep cleanup to a minimum, use paper liners inside each cupcake mold. They also help keep cupcakes from drying out. Plus, their color is a decoration!

Silicone muffin/cupcake pans are great for easy cleanup and longevity. Place them on a cookie sheet and make sure it is level.

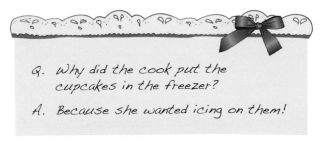

Q. Why did the cook put the cupcakes in the freezer?

A. Because she wanted icing on them!

Index

A

Articles

B

C

Chocolate Cupcakes and Frostings

They are called all sorts of things: patty cake papers, cupcake papers, muffin papers, cupcake liners. You know the little paper things you use to line cupcake pans or trays.

If you are looking for easy decorating then cupcake papers are the answer. They instantly add color and fun to any cupcake. Have a look around your local cake decorating store and you are sure to find heaps of fun prints and colors.

There is a time every day when the phones go unanswered, the TV is off and e-mails can wait. For this short time, you are family and it is your dinnertime.

Cookbooks Published by
Cookbook Resources, LLC
Bringing Family and Friends to the Table

The Best 1001 Short, Easy Recipes
1001 Slow Cooker Recipes
1001 Short, Easy, Inexpensive Recipes
1001 Fast Easy Recipes
1001 Community Recipes
Easy Slow Cooker Cookbook
Busy Woman's Slow Cooker Recipes
Busy Woman's Quick & Easy Recipes
Easy Diabetic Recipes
365 Easy Soups and Stews
365 Easy Chicken Recipes
365 Easy One-Dish Recipes
365 Easy Soup Recipes
365 Easy Vegetarian Recipes
365 Easy Casserole Recipes
365 Easy Pasta Recipes
365 Easy Slow Cooker Recipes
Leaving Home Cookbook and Survival Guide
Essential 3-4-5 Ingredient Recipes
Ultimate 4 Ingredient Cookbook
Easy Cooking with 5 Ingredients
The Best of Cooking with 3 Ingredients
Ultimate 4 Ingredient Diabetic Cookbook
4-Ingredient Recipes for 30-Minute Meals
Cooking with Beer
The Pennsylvania Cookbook
The California Cookbook
Best-Loved New England Recipes
Best-Loved Canadian Recipes
Best-Loved Recipes from the Pacific Northwest

Easy Slow Cooker Recipes (with Photos)
Cool Smoothies (with Photos)
Easy Cupcake Recipes (with Photos)
Easy Soup Recipes (with Photos)
Classic Tex-Mex and Texas Cooking
Best-Loved Southern Recipes
Classic Southwest Cooking
Miss Sadie's Southern Cooking
Classic Pennsylvania Dutch Cooking
Healthy Cooking with 4 Ingredients
Trophy Hunters' Wild Game Cookbook
Recipe Keeper
Simple Old-Fashioned Baking
Quick Fixes with Cake Mixes
Kitchen Keepsakes & More Kitchen Keepsakes
Cookbook 25 Years
Texas Longhorn Cookbook
Gifts for the Cookie Jar
All New Gifts for the Cookie Jar
The Big Bake Sale Cookbook
Easy One-Dish Meals
Easy Potluck Recipes
Easy Casseroles
Easy Desserts
Sunday Night Suppers
Easy Church Suppers
365 Easy Meals
Gourmet Cooking with 5 Ingredients
Muffins In A Jar
A Little Taste of Texas
A Little Taste of Texas II

cookbook
resources LLC
www.cookbookresources.com
Toll-Free 866-229-2665
Your Ultimate Source for Easy Cookbook

cookbook resources® LLC

www.cookbookresources.com

Toll free 1-866-229-2665

Your Ultimate Source for Easy Cookbooks